WHO LIKES BUGS? WE DO!

ANIMAL BOOK AGE 8

Children's Animal Books

Speedy Publishing LLC
40 E. Main St. #1156
Newark, DE 19711
www.speedypublishing.com
Copyright 2017

All Rights reserved. No part of this book may be reproduced or used in any way or form or by any means whether electronic or mechanical, this means that you cannot record or photocopy any material ideas or tips that are provided in this book.

•WOOD LANE COMMUNITY LIBRARY•
In memory of CindyHiscock
SN153EE

They crawl, they fly, they buzz near our ears! Let's learn about true bugs and what they do!

BUZZING AND CREEPING

Insects are everywhere-and that's a good thing. They help pollinate plants, they aerate the soil, they provide food for spiders and birds and fish and even some mammals! Insects are an essential part of the ecosystem of earth.

Fly

Sometimes they are annoying, especially when they get into our food or sting us. But we and they share this world, and most insect species were around long before humans appeared on the scene. So we need to learn to live with them and even appreciate them.

There are insects we know well, like ants, bees, and flies. There are other insects we may never see, because they live high up in trees or under the ground.

Bees

All insects have these things in common:

- They have a three-part body, with a head, a thorax, and an abdomen.

- They don't have a skeleton the way we do, inside the body. They have an "exoskeleton", a hard exterior shell, that protects what's inside and lets their legs and wings function.

- They have two antennae, compound eyes (not like our eyes), and three pairs of legs.

- They don't have a nose and lungs to get the oxygen their cells need. Instead, insects get air through tiny holes all along the sides of their bodies.

Ants

Ladybug

- In human bodies, our blood is inside a circulatory system of arteries and veins, and is pumped by a heart. In insects, the blood just sort of sloshes around inside the exoskeleton, with no system to deliver it and no heart to pump it.

NOT ALL INSECTS ARE BUGS

No matter which insect it is, we often call it a "bug". But for scientists, "bug" is a particular type of insect. All bugs are insects, but not all insects are bugs. Scientists sometimes call this sub-group "true bugs".

Black Fly

True bugs are part of the Hemiptera order of insects.

The insects themselves don't care what you call them, of course!

WHAT TRUE BUGS ARE LIKE

The most obvious feature all true bugs share is their mouth parts. True bugs don't have any way to bite or tear at their prey. Instead, they have a long, strong beak. They stab this beak into a plant, an insect, or an animal and suck liquid from inside it.

Assassin Bug

Here are some other features of true bugs:

- True bugs are usually warm-blooded.

- They are often parasites like bedbugs, or hunters like assassin bugs.

- They may have two pairs of wings. The front wings are thicker, almost like pieces of shell, and have colors close to the body. The outer edge of the wing may be clear. If they have hind wings, the wings are clear and tucked in under the front wings.

- When they are not flying or drying their wings, true bugs fold them so the hind wings, if any, are flat against the body and protected by the front wings.

- Real bugs have a three-stage "incomplete metamorphosis", compared to the "complete metamorphosis" of other insects. They go from eggs to larva or nymphs and then to adults, without going through the larval stage other insects go through.

Monarch Caterpillar

- The nymphs or larvae of real bugs may spend their time underground, near the surface of the ground, or underwater, depending on the species.

Shield Bugs

- True bugs have, along with their eyes, up to three ocelli. These are light-sensitive areas, like primitive eyes, that can help the bug detect movement and, when flying, where the horizon is.

MEET SOME TRUE BUGS

There are over 40,000 species of true bugs, and they live everywhere on Earth except in Antarctica. Here are some interesting ones:

Assassin Bug

There are over 7,000 species of assassin bugs. They hunt other insects. When they catch one, they stick their sharp beak into it and suck out the insides of their victim. A few species can actually hurt humans by transmitting diseases, but most assassin bugs are helpful to humans because they attack insects that eat our crops.

Assassin Bug

Stink Bug

Stink Bug

Stink bugs are also called shield bugs. They can squirt out a nasty smell when they are attacked. There are over five thousand species of stink bugs, and most of them are plant-eaters.

Water Strider

Water striders, or pond skaters, can walk on water! There are over 70 different species, all with special hairs at the ends of their legs. The hairs are water-repellent and spread out to make a little floatie for each leg of this true bug. They hunt and attack smaller insects, moving so quickly over the water that they seem to be skating.

Toe Biter

Toe Biter

There are over 150 kinds of toe biters. Some of them are among the largest true bugs, and grow as long as five inches!. They tend to live in small bodies of water, hiding under dead leaves. Toe biters are hunters, and often attack and kill insects, fish, salamanders, and frogs that are much larger than they are. Why do you think they are called "toe biters"? That's right: if you have bare feet in a pond or pool of water you may suddenly feel a painful sting on one of your toes. A toe biter is attacking!

Marine Skater

Marine skaters are like water striders, but they live on the ocean. They are able to slide from wave to wave without sinking. They lay their eggs on driftwood, seaweed, or other floating objects and let the eggs drift where they will until they hatch.

Marine Skater

Cicada

Cicada

Cicadas spend most of their lives as nymphs, living and eating underground. Then, every 13 or 17 years, depending on the species, they change into their adult form. Thousands of cicadas emerge at the same time to mate and create new babies. They make a very loud sound as they call to each other.

Giant Water Bug

Giant water bugs have an enlightened child-raising policy. The females lay their eggs on the back of a male giant water bug. The male takes care of the eggs until they hatch while the female goes on with her life.

Giant Water Bug

Water Scorpion

Water Scorpion

Water scorpions have long breathing tubes attached to the back end of their bodies. This lets them get air while most of the water scorpion is under water. They live happily in small ponds, or in water that is polluted and does not have much oxygen, because of their breathing tube.

Spittlebug

The spittlebug is also called the froghopper because it can jump long distances. But when they are nymphs they cover themselves with a protective froth of spittle. This helps keep them safe from predators while they feed on plants because it tastes bad, and insulates them from hot and cold weather. The spittle is sometimes called "cuckoo spit", "frog spit", or "snake spit", but it has nothing to do with any of those animals.

Kissing Bug

Kissing Bug

Kissing bugs get their name because their bite marks sometimes show up around people's mouths. They live on blood they suck from animals or people They hide during the day and come out to feed in the dark. Kissing bugs in the tropics can carry and transmit Chagas disease, which can be fatal. The usual reaction to their bites is extreme itchiness.

Harlequin Bug

Also known as the cabbage bug, calico bug, or fire bug, this true bug is a serious attacker of crops in the southern United States. If it is not controlled it can ruin an entire field of cabbages. After the bug has sucked a lot of sap out of a plant, the plant turns brown and shrivels up as it dies.

Harlequin Bug

Leaf Cutter Ants

COOL TRUE BUG FACTS

Here are some cool things to know about true bugs:

- The assassin bug kills ants and eats their insides. Then it piles some of the bodies on its own body to scare away larger bugs and even birds who might otherwise attack it.

- The red postman butterfly is poisonous to birds, so birds avoid eating them. It develops that poison by eating material from poisonous plants, and then storing the poison.

Postman Butterfly

- People use true bugs for both human and pet food. Chinese recipes sometimes include certain water bugs to add a special flavor to the dish! If you have a pet turtle and buy food for him from the pet shop, that food is made almost completely of small water bugs.

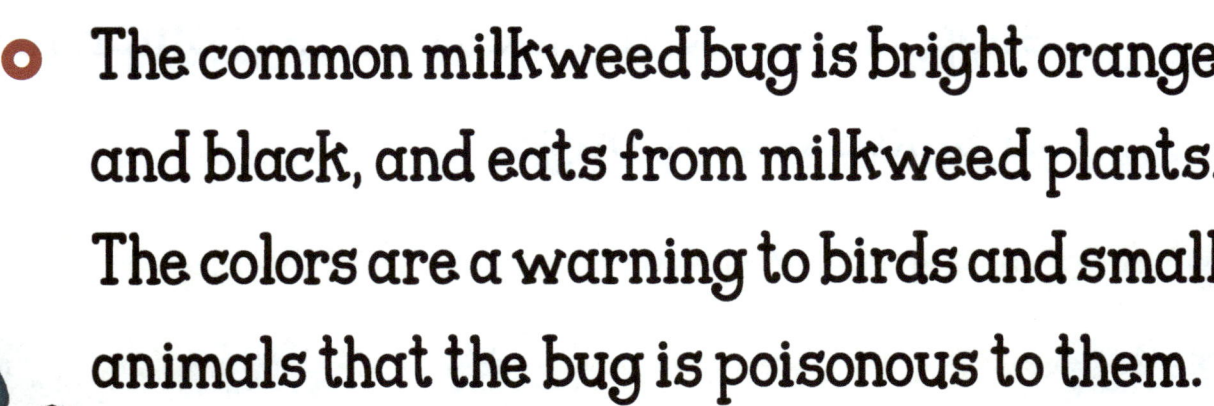

Milkweed Bug

- The common milkweed bug is bright orange and black, and eats from milkweed plants. The colors are a warning to birds and small animals that the bug is poisonous to them.

Assassin Bug

- Some assassin bugs can make hissing noises, possibly as a warning to scare off attackers. They make the sound by rubbing their feeding tube back and forth against their body.

Mosquito

- Mosquitoes love the smell of your feet when they get sweaty!

MORE ABOUT THE INSECTS AROUND YOU

Read Baby Professor books like Discovering Winged Insects and Insects and Arachnids to learn more about the small-and not-so-small- creatures who share this world with us.

Milton Keynes UK
Ingram Content Group UK Ltd.
UKHW051148030924
447802UK00003B/391